60

THE WORLD'S 60 BEST HEALTHY SMOOTHIES... PERIOD.

CÉLINE TRÉGAN & VÉRONIQUE PARADIS

PHOTOGRAPHER: Antoine Sicotte
ART DIRECTORS: Antoine Sicotte & Véronique Paradis
GRAPHIC DESIGNER: Laurie Auger
COVER DESIGNER: Laurie Auger
FOOD STYLIST: Véronique Paradis
ENGLISH TRANSLATOR: Lorien Jones
COPY EDITOR: Anna Phelan

PROJECT EDITOR: Antoine Ross Trempe

ISBN: 978-2-924155-08-0

Legal Deposit: 2012
Bibliothèque et Archives du Québec
Library and Archives Canada
ISBN: 978-2-924155-08-0

The publisher acknowledges the financial support of the Government of Canada through the Canada Book Fund (CBF) for its publishing activities and the support of the Government of Quebec through the tax credits for book publishing program (SODEC).

Originally published under the title
"Les 60 meilleurs smoothies santé du monde... Point final."

PRINTED IN CANADA

THE WORLD'S 60 BEST

HEALTHY SMOOTHIES

PERIOD.

THE WORLD'S 60 BEST

HEALTHY SMOOTHIES

PERIOD.

ABOUT THIS BOOK

The 60 smoothies in this book are, *in our opinion*, the 60 best smoothies in the world. Our team of chefs, writers and foodies explored everything the culinary world has to offer to create this collection of the world's 60 best smoothies.

We based our recipes on the following criteria:

QUALITY OF INGREDIENTS
ORIGINALITY
TASTE
APPEARANCE
SIMPLICITY

Are these our personal favorite smoothies? Of course! But rest assured, our team of passionate, dedicated gourmets put time and loving care into formulating and testing each recipe in order to provide you with the 60 best smoothies ever. In fact, our chef brought each freshly made smoothies straight from the kitchen into the studio—no colorants, no sprays, no special effects added—and after each photo shoot, our creative team got to enjoy the very smoothies you see in these photos.

We hope you'll enjoy discovering these recipes and using this book as much as we enjoyed making it.

TABLE OF CONTENTS

INTRO

Every one of the 60 best smoothies in this book features a flavor and cost legend (see pages 016 and 017) to guide your taste buds, as well as your wallet, in choosing the perfect smoothie according to your personal tastes, dietary needs, and budget. You'll also find a glossary of culinary terms (page 029), handy cooking tips and tricks (page 021), and a list of must-have kitchen tools (page 021) that will help you create the world's BEST smoothies. Finally, use the easy-to-follow table of contents (pages 010 and 011) and ingredients index (pages 176 to 179) to find everything you're looking for.

In this book you'll discover the health-giving benefits of each smoothie, interesting food facts from our "Did you know?" sidebars, and tasty variations. Above all, we want you to be inspired to try out different foods and flavor combinations to take your smoothies to the next level.

Bon appétit!

TANGY

SALTY

SWEET

DAIRY

COST

LEGEND

ACIDIC • LEMONY • VINEGARY

LOW

MEDIUM

HIGH

SALTY

LOW

MEDIUM

HIGH

SWEET

LOW

MEDIUM

HIGH

CONTAINS DAIRY

COST OF INGREDIENTS

LOW

MEDIUM

HIGH

A SHORT HISTORY OF SMOOTHIES

A smoothie is a blended beverage typically made with fresh fruit, fruit juice, and crushed ice, with a creamy, thick texture not unlike that of a milkshake. Most smoothies are sweet, and served cold.

The blender first appeared on the market in the 1930s, as a luxury item that few households could afford. Just a few decades later, specialty health food stores across the West Coast of the United States began selling puréed drinks using seasonal fruits and crushed ice, inspired by Brazilian recipes, which were closer in texture to slush or granita than the smoothies we know today.

By the 1960s and 1970s, most households owned freezers and were able to freeze seasonal fruit to be used throughout the year, and both health food and ice cream shops had started featuring smoothies as regular menu items. The health and fitness movement reached new heights in the 1980s, and soon, small, independently owned juice and smoothie bars were springing up across North America. The next few decades saw a growing interest in maintaining a healthy lifestyle and staying fit, and smoothies became popular with the health-conscious crowd who wanted a convenient, lower-calorie, vitamin- and nutrient-rich meal alternative. Big companies soon caught on and began advertising smoothies as health and energy drinks, and shortly after, the smoothie became a retail phenomenon.

Today, the word smoothie is used to describe any number of blended beverages: a smoothie can be thick and creamy, made with dairy, tofu, soy milk, or almond milk; it can be a simple blend of fresh fruit and ice, or a savory cocktail of nutrient-packed vegetables; it can have any number of added nutritional supplements depending on a person's dietary needs, including vitamins, protein, and fiber, and it can even replace a meal. Even though smoothies are sold in most fast food restaurants and coffee shops, the very best smoothies are made at home, with the very freshest ingredients. *The World's 60 Best Smoothies... Period* offers a collection of classic and original, sweet and savory smoothies, and EVERY single combination is healthy... and absolutely delicious!

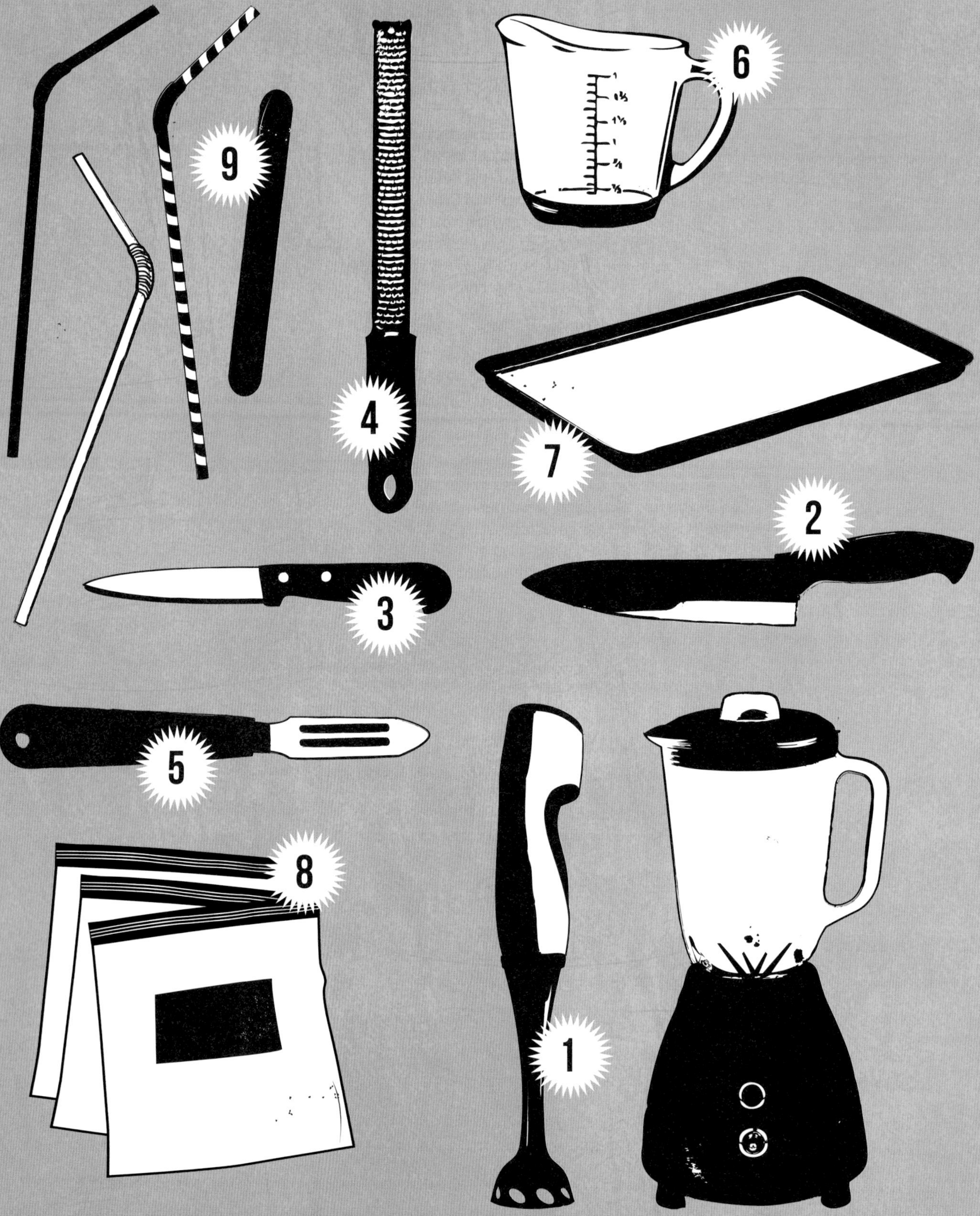
9
6
4
7
2
3
5
8
1

MUST-HAVE TOOLS

FOR THE WORLD'S BEST SMOOTHIES

1. A **blender or a hand blender** to purée delicious ingredients
2. A **chef's knife** for chopping, cubing, dicing, slicing, and mincing
3. A **small knife** for peeling smaller fruits and vegetables
4. A **zester or small grater** for zesting citrus fruits
5. A **peeler** for peeling fruits and vegetables
6. A **measuring cup** for measuring out exact quantities for perfectly balanced flavors
7. A **baking sheet** for freezing fruit
8. **Freezer bags** for storing fruit in the freezer and preventing freezer burn
9. **Straws and stir sticks** for a beautiful presentation

TIPS & TRICKS

FOR CREATING THE WORLD'S BEST SMOOTHIES

1. Easier to clean and more compact than a regular blender, a hand blender is the ultimate smoothie-making tool. Plus, it can be used for puréeing soups, dips, and pestos, and even for whipping up a batch of pancake batter!

2. Always use ripe fruit to make your smoothies: the riper it is, the sweeter and juicier it will be. Often, you won't even have to add any additional sweeteners like sugar or honey, saving you calories.

3. Stock your freezer with frozen fruit. Instead of throwing it away, freeze any overripe fruit, especially seasonal fruit, before it spoils: spread it out on a baking sheet, put it in the freezer, and, once frozen, transfer it to freezer bags. You'll have fruit available for making smoothies year-round.

4. Bananas ripen very quickly. Try storing them in the freezer—when you're ready to make your smoothies, just microwave them for about twenty seconds and peel! Frozen bananas are also an excellent substitute for crushed ice, and will add extra creaminess and sweetness.

5. Rehydrating dried fruit in advance will result in a creamier, less chunky smoothie. Simply heat a cup of water in the microwave, add the dried fruit, and soak for thirty minutes.

6. Crushed ice is the best ice for smoothies, but you can also use ice cubes if you have a powerful enough blender. If you're using a hand blender, first put the ice cubes into a plastic freezer bag and crush with a hard object. Or, instead of crushed ice, use sherbet, ice cream, or frozen fruit!

7. Smoothies can be kept up to twenty-four hours in the refrigerator before the fruit starts to oxidize. Prepare a pitcher for the whole family to drink for breakfast or at a midday snack.

8. There's nothing better on a hot summer day than a sweet frozen treat! Turn your smoothies into healthy popsicles: just pour into molds or paper cups and insert a popsicle stick or spoon into each. Freeze and enjoy!

9. Are your savory appetizer smoothies missing a bit of bite? Add a splash of white wine or vodka to impress your guests with original cocktails.

10. Finally, remember that the best recipes are made with the freshest ingredients. Eat fresh!

HEALTH GUIDE

FRUIT	HEALTH BENEFITS
APPLE	Eating the skin of the apple, which is richer in vitamin C than the flesh, is highly recommended, but it must be thoroughly washed beforehand. This fruit has many health-giving virtues: it provides energy, lowers cholesterol, and provides a feeling of fullness thanks to its high fiber and water content, making the apple the perfect snack for those looking to maintain a healthy weight. The apple is also very rich in pectin, which limits and delays the absorption of sugar by the blood and helps curb hunger.
APRICOT	The apricot helps fight fatigue and depression. It is high in potassium, is a good source of vitamins C, B1, B2, B5, and PP, and is rich in sugar, mineral nutrients, and many trace elements, which contribute to the fruit's antianemic and antiasthenic properties.
AVOCADO	The avocado is beneficial to the stomach and intestines, and is an excellent source of potassium and folate, a good source of vitamin B6, and contains magnesium, pantothenic acid, vitamin C, copper, niacin, iron, vitamin A, and zinc.
BANANA	The banana contains antioxidants, and its phospholipids and pectin help prevent the development of ulcers in the stomach's mucous membrane. It is also rich in calories, fiber, and cramp-fighting potassium.
BLACKBERRY	The blackberry is a good source of vitamin C and potassium, and contains magnesium and copper. It also has antihemorrhagic properties.
BLUEBERRY	This antibacterial berry is recommended in cases of gastroenteritis and cystitis, and to protect blood vessels. It is also a good source of vitamin C, potassium, and fiber.
CHERRY	Possessing remineralising, diuretic, antiarthritic, and antirheumatic properties, this slightly laxative fruit is recognized for its cleansing virtues. Both sweet and sour cherries contain potassium, but sour cherries are slightly higher in this digestion-stimulating elecrolyte.
CRANBERRY	The cranberry is widely used to help treat urinary infections and to correct circulatory system deficiencies. It also contains vitamin C and potassium.
CURRANT	This strength-giving berry is often recommended to help slow the onset of osteoporosis. It also stimulates the appetite and digestion.
DATE	Ultra-nutritious, the date helps renew red blood cells. Dried dates are a source of copper, pantothenic acid, vitamin B6, niacin, magnesium, and iron.
FIG	The fig is diuretic and laxative. Fresh figs are a good source of potassium, magnesium, iron, and copper, and a source of fiber.

FRUIT	HEALTH BENEFITS
GOJI BERRY	The Goji berry contains high concentrations of vitamin C and is very rich in antioxidants, elements that help prevent diseases associated with aging.
GRAPE	Rich in pigments and tannins, the grape been shown to help strengthen the walls of the smaller blood vessels. The grape is also a heart-healthy food thanks to its high concentration of polyphenols, protective pigments that help keep the cardiovascular system in good shape. However, due to its high sugar content, it is quite high in calories.
GRAPEFRUIT	The grapefruit is rich in vitamin C and is a good source of potassium. It is also diuretic and tonic, and protects capillaries and weak blood vessels.
GUAVA	Guava is a source of vitamin C, and accelerates the healing of skin wounds. Its fiber prevents constipation and regulates the bowels.
KIWI	An excellent source of vitamin C and potassium, the kiwi is diuretic and laxative and is a recommended food in the prevention of cardiovascular issues.
LEMON	The lemon is a diuretic, and one of the most effective natural antiseptics. Recognized for its high vitamin C content, it also contains potassium and folate.
MANGO	The mango contains high concentrations of vitamins A and C, and restores health and detoxifies the liver. Its antioxidant properties are well known.
MELON	The melon provides provitamin A (carotene), and is rich in vitamins C and B, as well as in various trace elements and fiber.
ORANGE	Best known for its wealth of vitamin C, the orange is often recommended in cases of hypertension, anorexia, and shortness of breath. This citrus fruit is low in calories, contains fiber and calcium, and is renowned for helping to reinforce the body's natural defenses against respiratory ailments, the flu, and other similar viruses, by stimulating the immune system.
PAPAYA	Papaya is a source of vitamin C, potassium, and vitamin A. Its precious enzyme (papain) promotes protein digestion.
PEACH	The peach is very rich in fiber, hydrates the body, and contains potassium, calcium, vitamin C, and magnesium.
PEAR	The pear helps prevent osteoporosis and, like its relative the apple, hydrates and provides a good source of fiber, promoting healthy intestinal transit.
PINEAPPLE	Most of the pineapple's sugars are concentrated in its outer skin. The pineapple is high in fiber, potassium, vitamin C, magnesium, and carotene, acts as an antiseptic and an intestinal anti-inflammatory agent, and helps fight arteriosclerosis.

FRUIT	HEALTH BENEFITS
PLUM	The plum contains vitamins C, B, and E, as well as potassium. This fruit is recommended in cases of constipation and food poisoning, and contains a large amount of fiber, water, and sorbitol, which, together, make an effective laxative.
POMEGRANATE	Three times richer in antioxidants than green tea, this red fruit helps fight cell oxidation and slows the skin's aging process.
RASPBERRY	The raspberry is a good source of vitamin C, potassium, magnesium, and fiber. A natural diuretic and heart strengthener, this berry also relieves heartburn and constipation. The raspberry bush's leaves, when infused as a tea, have astringent, diuretic, and laxative properties.
STRAWBERRY	This berry contains vitamin C, potassium, folate, pantothenic acid, and magnesium, and stimulates the system's defenses against infections. It is also known as an effective tonic, purgative, diuretic, and astringent.
TOMATO	The tomato is an excellent source of vitamin C, as well as carotene and vitamin E, which stimulate the body's natural defenses. It is also high in dietary minerals and trace elements, most notably potassium, which plays a role in regulating kidney function.

LIQUID	HEALTH BENEFITS
ALMOND MILK	Gluten free and rich in fiber and protein, this milk is one of the best sources of the antioxidant vitamin E, which helps to slow down cellular and cutaneous aging.
COW'S MILK	This milk contains very important proteins (each containing essential amino acids), high levels of calcium and vitamin D (which helps prevents rickets), and is rich in riboflavin, vitamin A, magnesium, and fatty acids, including omega-3 and omega-6 fatty acids.
OAT MILK	Oat milk is lactose and cholesterol free. It contains beta-glucans that reduce bad cholesterol and promote intestinal transit.
RICE MILK	Rice milk does not impact blood sugar levels and is rich in slow sugars. Like oat milk, rice milk has a very neutral taste.
SOY MILK	The low levels of saturated amino acids in this beverage help regulate the body's cholesterol level.
YOGURT	Yogurt is an excellent source of protein, calcium, phosphorous, potassium, and vitamins A and B. Plain, unsweetened yogurt's nutritional value is very close to that of the milk used to prepare it. It restores the intestinal flora after an antibiotic treatment and, when eaten before bed, encourages sleep.

VEGETABLE	HEALTH BENEFITS
BASIL	Basil is packed with healing vitamin C and antioxidant vitamin A. It also clears the respiratory passages and acts as an antiseptic.
BEET	The beet is unique in that it contains extremely high levels of carotenoids. Rich in carbohydrates and low in fat, it is also loaded with antioxidants that help the body fight heart disease and certain cancers.
BROCCOLI	Broccoli has one of the highest levels of vitamin C out of all of green vegetables. It supplies antioxidant provitamin A and vitamin B9, which helps reduce the risk of colon cancer.
CARROT	The carrot is an excellent source of provitamin A. Its antioxidant compounds help protect against cardiovascular diseases and cancer, and promote healthy vision.
CUCUMBER	This crunchy vegetable is an effective purgative and diuretic. It is a source of many vitamins, the B complex vitamins in particular, and its skin contains provitamin A and vitamin E, which helps slow cellular aging.
GINGER	Ginger can lower blood pressure and increase circulation thanks to the gingerol it contains. It also helps relieve motion sickness and morning sickness.
MINT	Long known for its calming, analgesic, and anasthetic virtues, mint not only soothes pain, it can also be used as a respiratory and digestive antiseptic.
PARSLEY	Parsley is very rich in antioxidant vitamin C and carotene (provitamin A). It helps fight anemia and possesses healing and stimulating properties.
PUMPKIN	The pumpkin contains cancer-fighting carotenoids. The vitamins in the pumpkin help protect against cardiovascular diseases.
RED PEPPER	The red pepper is an excellent source of carotene (provitamin A) and flavonoids, both found in its pigments. Carotene is an antioxidant and helps prevent premature cellular aging; flavonoids protect the capillaries. The riper and redder the pepper, the more of these precious pigments it contains.
SPINACH	Spinach's green leaves are positively bursting with minerals. It also contains iron and powerful antioxidants that protect the body against the premature aging of cells, reinforces vitamin C's immunity-boosting action, and protects the capillaries.

1
2
3
4
5
6
7
8
9

GLOSSARY

1. SEASON

To improve the flavor of a dish by adding salt and pepper to taste.

2. PEEL

To remove the outer layer, peel, or skin of a fruit or vegetable using a small knife or peeler.

3. PEEL AND SEGMENT

To remove the peel, pith, and inner membranes of a citrus fruit, leaving only the pulp. The easiest way to peel and segment citrus fruit? Cut off both ends, place it on a flat work surface, and cut downwards, underneath the white pith, around the entire fruit.

4. STRAIN

To pour through a wire mesh strainer in order to separate liquid food from solid food, which results in a silky-smooth beverage.

5. SEED

To remove the seeds from certain fruits and vegetables using a small spoon.

6. ZEST

To remove the zest, or outer peel, of citrus fruits with a zester, grater, or paring knife.

7. PURÉE

To process food in a blender, or with a hand blender, until very smooth.

8. HULL

To remove the stem and leaves of certain fruits (such as strawberries).

9. WILT

To cook certain vegetables (spinach, Swiss chard, kale, sorrel, etc.) over low heat, with or without a fat, in order to reduce their volume and release some of their liquid.

THE CHEF'S SECRET

Every seasoned chef will attest that the real secret to creating a successful dish is to *taste! taste! taste!* Taste before and after seasoning, add some heat or a squeeze of lemon juice if you think your dish needs a little kick, or go ahead and double the herbs or even the cheese! The most important thing is to follow your instincts and your senses. Listen for that telltale sizzle, inhale the tantalizing aromas, and CONSTANTLY taste your food so you can get to know your dish in all its stages.

There you have it—the simple secret to creating delicious, original dishes.

1

CREAMY PEANUT

1 SERVING

INGREDIENTS

1 cup (250 ml) almond milk
1 tbsp peanut butter
1/2 cup (125 ml) vanilla yogurt
2 tbsp oat bran

PREPARATION

In a blender, or with a hand blender, purée all ingredients until smooth. Serve.

2

AVOCADO & GREEN APPLE

1 SERVING

INGREDIENTS

1/2 cup (125 ml) water
1 green apple, cored, peeled, and quartered
1/2 ripe avocado, peeled
1 tbsp lime juice

PREPARATION

In a blender, or with a hand blender, purée all ingredients until smooth. Drink immediately.

HEALTH BENEFITS

Avocados are an excellent source of antioxidants. They also help protect the heart and prevent strokes.

3

PLUMMY GRAPE

1 SERVING

INGREDIENTS

1/2 cup (125 ml) orange juice
1/2 banana
1 black plum, pitted
10 to 15 green or red seedless grapes

PREPARATION

In a blender, or with a hand blender, pulse ingredients until smooth. Drink immediately.

4

GAZPACHO SMOOTHIE

2 SERVINGS

INGREDIENTS

1 cup (250 ml) tomato juice
6 slices cucumber, peeled
1 roasted red pepper
Salt and freshly ground pepper

PREPARATION

In a blender, or with a hand blender, pulse ingredients until smooth. Serve immediately.

HEALTH BENEFITS

Red peppers are rich in vitamin C and an excellent source of carotene and flavonoids, powerful antioxidants that prevent the premature aging of cells.

5

SWEET ALMOND & APRICOT

1 SERVING

INGREDIENTS

1/2 cup (125 ml) almond milk
1/2 fresh or frozen banana
4 dried apricots
1 tbsp lemon juice

PREPARATION

In a blender, or with a hand blender, purée all ingredients until smooth. Drink immediately.

HEALTH BENEFITS

Certain experts believe that a diet rich in magnesium can help fight headaches. Some magnesium-rich foods include bananas, dates, dried apricots, avocados, almonds, and cashews.

DID YOU KNOW?

Although the apricot originated in China, today, Mediterranean countries, as well as Iran, are the world's leading apricot producers.

6

SPARKLING MELON

1 SERVING

INGREDIENTS

1 cup (250 ml) watermelon, seeded and cut into pieces
1/2 apple, peeled and cut into pieces
1 tbsp lemon juice
Zest of 1 lemon
1/2 cup (125 ml) sodium-free sparkling water

PREPARATION

In a blender, purée all ingredients, except sparkling water, until smooth. Pour in sparkling water and mix with a spoon. Drink immediately.

HEALTH BENEFITS

Watermelon is loaded with antioxidants (lycopene and carotenoids) that boost blood circulation, and the vitamin C it contains plays a vital role in collagen production.

DID YOU KNOW?

Sparkling water (sometimes called seltzer) is actually just water to which carbon dioxide has been added.

7

BLUE SERENITY

2 SERVINGS

INGREDIENTS

1 cup (250 ml) lemon balm infusion, chilled
1 cup (250 ml) frozen blueberries
1 frozen banana
1/2 cup (125 ml) baby spinach
1 tbsp almond butter
1 tbsp flaxseed oil

PREPARATION

To prepare the lemon balm infusion, boil 1 cup (250 ml) water and add 1 tsp dried lemon balm leaves. Let steep, strain, and then chill liquid. If desired, chill the infusion in an ice cube tray and use in your drinks and smoothies. You can also substitute the infusion with almond milk or plain yogurt.

In a blender, or with a hand blender, pulse ingredients until smooth. Serve.

HEALTH BENEFITS

Blueberries provide vitamin C as well as potassium, which keeps the nervous system functioning optimally. Bananas are high in calming B vitamins, and spinach, for its part, is a good source of folate, vitamin B6, iron, potassium, and magnesium, all essential nutrients that help combat stress. Almonds are rich in vitamin E and calcium and help lower cholesterol, while lemon balm strengthens the nervous system.

DID YOU KNOW?

Known by the Ancient Greeks to have beneficial properties, lemon balm is now used medicinally and as a flavoring for ice cream and herbal teas.

8

THE FIGHTER

1 SERVING

INGREDIENTS

1 orange
1/2 cup (125 ml) cantaloupe, peeled and cut into pieces
1 cup (250 ml) fresh pineapple, peeled, cored, and cut into cubes
7 blanched almonds or 1 tbsp almond flour
1/4 cup (60 ml) probiotic yogurt
1/2 cup (125 ml) crushed ice

PREPARATION

In a blender, or with a hand blender, purée all ingredients until smooth. If mixture is too thick, add a bit of fresh orange juice. Serve immediately.

HEALTH BENEFITS

As everyone knows, oranges and pineapples are extremely rich in vitamin C, a powerful antioxidant that helps heal wounds and form scar tissue, and boosts the immune system. Melon provides vitamin A, and almonds supply vitamin E. As an added bonus, the probiotics in the yogurt restore essential intestinal flora.

DID YOU KNOW?

From a botanical point of view, the pineapple isn't one single fruit! It's actually multiple berries that have fused together—each hexagonal "eye" was once a flower.

9

BROCCOLI BOOST

1 SERVING

INGREDIENTS

3 broccoli florets, cooked al dente
1/2 green apple, cored, peeled, and quartered
1/2 cup (125 ml) orange juice
1 tsp real maple syrup

PREPARATION

In a blender, or with a hand blender, purée all ingredients until smooth. If mixture is too thick, add a bit of water.

HEALTH BENEFITS

Broccoli, in the cruciferous family (cabbage, kale, Brussels sprouts, spinach, cauliflower), is a detoxifying food, and can be eaten in large quantities without worrying about weight gain. It contains both vitamin C and sulfurous derivatives that help eliminate toxins from the liver.

10

BEET WITH A BITE

2 SERVINGS

INGREDIENTS

1 medium red beet, cooked, peeled, and quartered
1/2 cup (125 ml) fresh grapefruit juice
Juice of 2 oranges
1 tbsp fresh ginger, peeled and grated
1 tbsp cane syrup or sugar

PREPARATION

In a blender, or with a hand blender, pulse ingredients until smooth. Serve.

HEALTH BENEFITS

Beets and citrus fruits are excellent cancer-fighting foods, and ginger activates the immune system.

DID YOU KNOW?

In Europe, the white beet, commonly known as the sugar beet, is grown commercially for sugar production and to make molasses and even vodka.

11

BANANA MANGOSTEEN

2 SERVINGS

INGREDIENTS

1/2 banana
3 mangosteens, peeled
1 cup (250 ml) pineapple juice
1 tbsp real maple syrup

PREPARATION

In a blender, or with a hand blender, purée all ingredients until smooth. Serve.

HEALTH BENEFITS

Pineapples contain bromelain, while bananas are alkalizing and the mangosteen has antioxidant properties. The perfect cocktail to help relieve joint pain caused by arthritis!

DID YOU KNOW?

The mangosteen is a round, purplish fruit, about the size of a golf ball. Its rind, or exocarp, is thick, bitter, and inedible, and its sweet, tangy white flesh is divided into four to eight segments.

12

POMEGRANATE POWER

1 SERVING

INGREDIENTS

1 pomegranate
1 tbsp honey
1/2 cup (125 ml) frozen strawberries

PREPARATION

Cut pomegranate into 4 pieces and, using a spoon, scoop out seeds into a bowl. Place all ingredients in a blender and blend for 30 seconds. Strain with a wire mesh strainer and serve immediately. If desired, add 1/2 cup (125 ml) soy milk.

HEALTH BENEFITS

Women's cholesterol levels rise sharply around menopause, increasing the risk of various diseases. Pomegranates, as well as berries, are high in anthocyanins and help lower cholesterol levels.

13

CARDIO COCKTAIL

2 SERVINGS

INGREDIENTS

2 peaches or nectarines, pitted and cut into pieces
1/2 cup (125 ml) berries of your choice
(strawberries, raspberries, blackberries, etc.)
1/4 cup (60 ml) plain yogurt
1 tbsp honey
4 fresh mint leaves
1 cup (250 ml) crushed ice

PREPARATION

In a blender, or with a hand blender, purée all ingredients until smooth. Serve.

HEALTH BENEFITS

The polyphenols found in berries contribute to cardiovascular health and improve the elasticity of the blood vessel walls.

LITRE
1000
1
750
3/4
500
1/2

14

BERRY ENERGY

2 SERVINGS

INGREDIENTS

1 cup (250 ml) plain soy milk
1 banana
1 orange
1/2 cup (125 ml) fresh or frozen raspberries
1 tsp fresh ginger, peeled and grated
1/2 cup (125 ml) crushed ice

PREPARATION

In a blender, or with a hand blender, purée all ingredients until smooth. Serve.

HEALTH BENEFITS

This smoothie is rich in vitamin C. To boost immunity, drink one per day for two weeks, for breakfast or as a snack.

DID YOU KNOW?

In the Middle Ages, ginger was extremely expensive: just one pound could buy an entire live sheep!

15

TOTAL TOFU

2 SERVINGS

INGREDIENTS

1/4 cup (60 ml) coconut milk
1 cup (250 ml) orange juice
1 cup (250 ml) soft tofu, drained
1 fresh or frozen banana
1 cup (250 ml) fresh pineapple, peeled, cored, and cut into cubes

PREPARATION

In a blender, or with a hand blender, purée all ingredients until smooth. Serve.

VARIATION

Use soy milk instead of orange juice, and if you don't like pineapple, replace it with 1 cup (250 ml) fresh or frozen mango.

HEALTH BENEFITS

Drink this tasty smoothie for breakfast to jump-start your day, and for an extra energy boost, pair it with a slice of whole-wheat toast and a few fresh-cut raw veggies.

DID YOU KNOW?

Soft tofu, also known as silken tofu, should be stored in water and will keep in the refrigerator for 7 to 10 days. Change the tofu water daily.

16

MORNING DELIGHT

1 SERVING

INGREDIENTS

1/3 cup (80 ml) fresh berries of your choice
(strawberries, raspberries, blueberries, etc.)
1/2 cup (125 ml) milk
1 tsp honey
1 tbsp oat bran

PREPARATION

In a blender, or with a hand blender,, combine berries, milk, and honey. Add oat bran and let sit for 1 or 2 minutes. Blend again and serve immediately.

HEALTH BENEFITS

This breakfast is a real winner! It's quick and easy to make, and combines a quartet of fortifying foods: milk to promote healthy bones; fruit to provide essential vitamins; honey for energy; and oat bran as a source of fiber. Add a bowl of cereal or a muffin for an energizing morning meal!

17

REVITALIZING SMOOTHIE

1 SERVING

INGREDIENTS

1 grapefruit, peeled and segmented
1 apple, cored and quartered
1/2 cup (125 ml) almond milk
1 tbsp fresh ginger, peeled and grated
4 fresh mint leaves

PREPARATION

In a blender, or with a hand blender, purée all ingredients until smooth. Garnish with mint leaves.

HEALTH BENEFITS

Apples, rich in pectin and fiber, help flush out toxins and eliminate waste through the urine, while grapefruit has a natural laxative effect.

18

COCOA FUSION

1 SERVING

INGREDIENTS

1 cup (250 ml) almond milk
1/2 cup (125 ml) fresh or frozen raspberries
1/2 cup (125 ml) fresh or frozen blackberries
1 tbsp cocoa powder
Crushed ice (optional)

PREPARATION

In a blender, or with a hand blender, purée all ingredients until smooth. If fruit is fresh, add crushed ice before blending. Drink immediately.

HEALTH BENEFITS

Cocoa, nuts, and almonds are all rich in magnesium, a mineral that improves memory and helps fight stress.

DID YOU KNOW?

Each one of the cacao tree's pods, or fruits, contains 30 to 50 seeds, and about 400 seeds are needed to make one pound of chocolate.

19

MANGO, GUAVA & COCONUT

2 SERVINGS

INGREDIENTS

2 guavas, peeled and quartered
1 mango, peeled and diced
1/4 cup (60 ml) coconut milk
1 pinch nutmeg
Juice and zest of 1 lime
1 cup (250 ml) crushed ice

PREPARATION

In a blender, or with a hand blender, purée guava and diced mango. Add coconut milk, nutmeg, lime juice and zest, and crushed ice, and purée until smooth.

HEALTH BENEFITS

This exotic cocktail protects the heart thanks to its high concentration of antioxidants, and the guava helps lower cholesterol levels as well as arterial tension.

DID YOU KNOW?

The guava has been cultivated for over 2,000 years.

20

BLUEBERRY EXPLOSION

1 SERVING

INGREDIENTS

1 cup (250 ml) pomegranate juice
1 cup (250 ml) blueberries
1 tbsp honey

PREPARATION

In a blender, or with a hand blender, purée all ingredients until smooth. If mixture is too thick, add a bit more pomegranate juice.

VARIATION

Use cane sugar or real maple syrup instead of honey!

HEALTH BENEFITS

The antioxidant activity of pomegranates is higher than that of red wine, and even green tea, which helps protect the body against damage caused by free radicals. The fruit is also well known for its anti-inflammatory effects.

21

PEAR, KIWI & PINEAPPLE

2 SERVINGS

INGREDIENTS

2 pears, cored and cut into pieces
1 kiwi, peeled and cut into pieces
1 cup (250 ml) fresh pineapple, peeled, cored, and cut into pieces

PREPARATION

In a blender, or with a hand blender, purée all ingredients until smooth. Add water as needed. Serve.

HEALTH BENEFITS

Save your pear and apple peels: they contain precious cancer-fighting flavonoids and phenolic acids! Kiwis are packed with fiber, and a diet rich in fiber helps prevent cardiovascular diseases and certain types of cancer, and regulates the appetite.

DID YOU KNOW?

The kiwifruit originated in China, and before the 1950s was commonly known as the Chinese gooseberry. After the war, it was renamed by New Zealand exporters. The fruit's fuzzy exterior reminded them of the plumage of their national symbol: the kiwi, a small, brown, flightless bird.

22

SWEET DREAMS SMOOTHIE

1 SERVING

INGREDIENTS

1 cup (250 ml) oat milk
1/3 cup (80 ml) plain yogurt
1/2 banana
3 tbsp oats
2 drops vanilla extract

PREPARATION

In a blender, or with a hand blender, purée all ingredients until smooth. Drink before bedtime.

HEALTH BENEFITS

Warning: Oats are not recommended for people who are following a gluten-free diet.

Oats contain tryptophan, an amino acid essential to protein production. Tryptophan also helps control the appetite and regulates the sleep cycle, as well as the mood.

DID YOU KNOW?

The vanilla bean is actually the ripened fruit of a variety of orchid, and can be used whole, as an extract, and in powder form.

23

THE GUILT-FREE TREAT

1 SERVING

INGREDIENTS

2 fresh figs, quartered
1 pear, left unpeeled, cored and cut into pieces
1/2 cup (125 ml) plain yogurt
1/2 cup (125 ml) milk

PREPARATION

In a blender, or with a hand blender, purée all ingredients until smooth. Serve.

HEALTH BENEFITS

One fresh fig has about 25 calories—the perfect dessert for anyone following a weight loss plan. This fiber-rich fruit is highly recommended to help relieve constipation, and contains various minerals, B vitamins, and anthocyanins, which play a vital role in maintaining blood vessel health. Pears, for their part, are low in calories, have a high water content, and surpass most other foods in their level of folate, which supports neuromuscular function.

24

PAPAYA PASSION

2 SERVINGS

INGREDIENTS

1 cup (250 ml) orange juice
1/4 papaya, peeled and seeded
2 passion fruits, seeds only
1/2 cup (125 ml) crushed ice

PREPARATION

In a blender, or with a hand blender, pulse all ingredients until smooth. Serve immediately.

HEALTH BENEFITS

Papaya contains papain, an enzyme that facilitates digestion and soothes upset stomachs, while passion fruit helps prevent constipation. A fiber-rich diet lowers the risk of colon cancer and offsets hunger by increasing the feeling of fullness.

25

HAZELNUT ALMOND FLOAT

2 SERVINGS

INGREDIENTS

1/4 cup (60 ml) hazelnuts, blanched
3 tbsp ground almonds
1 cup (250 ml) milk
1 tbsp real maple syrup

PREPARATION

Mix together hazelnuts, ground almonds, and milk. Refrigerate for 10 to 15 minutes.

In a blender, or with a hand blender, purée all ingredients until smooth. Serve.

HEALTH BENEFITS

Nuts are a good source of melatonin and contain vitamin E, which helps keep the heart, brain, muscles, joints, eyes, skin, digestive system, and immune system healthy.

26

PUMPKIN POTION

2 SERVINGS

INGREDIENTS

Juice of 3 oranges, or 1 cup (250 ml) orange juice
1 cup (250 ml) pumpkin flesh, cooked
1 apple, cored and cut into pieces

PREPARATION

To cook the pumpkin, start by thoroughly washing it. Cut pumpkin in two and scoop out seeds. Place, cut sides down, on an oiled baking sheet and cook in a 375°F (190°C) for 1 hour, or until tender. Let cool. With a spoon, scoop out pumpkin flesh.

In a blender, or with a hand blender, pulse all ingredients until smooth. Serve.

HEALTH BENEFITS

The pumpkin is very rich in provitamin A (or beta-carotene), a major antioxidant that plays a role in preventing cancer, increasing immunity, and improving arteriosclerosis. In addition, the pumpkin is rich in inulin, a probiotic that stimulates the development of the intestinal flora. Pumpkin oil (very common in Austria) helps enlarge the prostate.

DID YOU KNOW?

Pumpkin seeds can be saved and eaten as a delicious snack! Just rinse and dry the seeds, and then drizzle them with oil and sprinkle with salt. Cook in a 350°F (175°C) oven for 10 to 15 minutes, or until crispy.

Squash was one of the three main plants grown by Native Americans. Maize (corn) and beans completed the trio, also called "The Three Sisters."

27

STRAWBERRY APPLE

3 SERVINGS

INGREDIENTS

1 cup (250 ml) pure apple juice (not from concentrate)
12 strawberries, hulled
4 red apples, peeled, cored, and cut into pieces
Crushed ice
1 tbsp real maple syrup or honey

PREPARATION

In a blender, or with a hand blender, pulse together apple juice, strawberries, apples, and crushed ice, until smooth. Add maple syrup and continue puréeing until creamy. Serve.

28

VITALITY COCKTAIL

1 SERVING

INGREDIENTS

1/4 cup (60 ml) orange juice
10 strawberries, hulled
3 tbsp plain yogurt
1 tbsp ground flaxseeds
2 tbsp pumpkin seeds, shelled
1/2 cup (125 ml) crushed ice

PREPARATION

In a blender, or with a hand blender, purée all ingredients until smooth. Serve.

HEALTH BENEFITS

Pumpkin seeds are a reputed health-boosting food, and are especially well known for helping to maintain a healthy prostate! These tasty seeds contain nutrients that promote testosterone production, and are extremely rich in zinc, an essential element for healthy sex organs.

DID YOU KNOW?

Canada is the world's top producer of flax.

29

FIGGY FIBER FIESTA

2 SERVINGS

INGREDIENTS

1 cup (250 ml) apple juice
2 plums, pitted
1/2 banana
2 dried figs
1/2 cup (125 ml) crushed ice

PREPARATION

In a blender, or with a hand blender, purée all ingredients until smooth. Serve.

HEALTH BENEFITS

Many types of fruit (including plums and figs) contain fiber, which helps prevent and relieve constipation.

DID YOU KNOW?

The fig was one of the first plants to be cultivated by humans, with evidence dating back to about 9400-9200 BCE!

30

THE BIG BLUE

2 SERVINGS

INGREDIENTS

1 cup (250 ml) grape juice
1 cup (250 ml) blueberries
1/2 cup (125 ml) plain yogurt
1/2 banana

PREPARATION

In a blender, or with a hand blender, purée all ingredients until smooth. Serve.

HEALTH BENEFITS

Studies have shown that the natural pigments (anthocyanins and flavonols) in blueberries and grapes help improve memory.

31

TASTE OF THE TROPICS

2 SERVINGS

INGREDIENTS

1 cup (250 ml) green tea, infused
1/4 cup (60 ml) coconut milk or plain yogurt
Juice of 1/2 lemon
1 cup (250 ml) fresh pineapple, peeled, cored, and cut into pieces
1 tsp fresh ginger, peeled and grated
1/2 cup (125 ml) crushed ice

PREPARATION

To prepare the green tea, infuse 1-1/2 tsp green tea leaves in 1 cup (250 ml) boiling water for 1 to 5 minutes. Let cool.

In a blender, or with a hand blender, purée all ingredients until smooth. Serve.

HEALTH BENEFITS

Theanine is a unique amino acid found in green tea that increases seratonin and dopamine levels in the brain. Pineapple and mango are rich in vitamin C, and ginger is a powerful antioxidant.

32

VELVETY TOMATO & BASIL

1 SERVING

INGREDIENTS

2 tomatoes, peeled and chopped
1/2 shallot, finely chopped
1/2 cup (125 ml) plain goat's milk yogurt
A few fresh basil leaves
Salt and freshly ground pepper

PREPARATION

In a blender, or with a hand blender, purée all ingredients until smooth. Serve as an appetizer or as a nutritious snack!

HEALTH BENEFITS

The proteins and fats in goat's milk and goat's milk products are easier to digest than the same products made with cow's milk.

DID YOU KNOW?

If you'd prefer to peel your tomatoes for an even creamier smoothie, plunge them in boiling water for 30 seconds to loosen the skin and make peeling a snap!

33

STRAWBERRY IMMUNITY

1 SERVING

INGREDIENTS

1/2 cup (125 ml) green tea, infused and chilled
1 cup (250 ml) fresh or frozen strawberries
1/4 cup (60 ml) soft tofu or plain soy milk
1 tbsp maple syrup or cane syrup
1/2 cup (125 ml) crushed ice (optional)

PREPARATION

To prepare the green tea, infuse 1-1/2 tsp green tea leaves in 1 cup (250 ml) boiling water for 1 to 5 minutes.

In a blender, or with a hand blender, pulse all ingredients until smooth.

HEALTH BENEFITS

The vitamin C found in strawberries strengthens the immune system and is a powerful, quick-acting antioxidant. One particular compound found in green tea is believed to play a key role in immune system health by increasing the number of certain beneficial cells. Soy is an excellent source of zinc, another nutrient responsible for the proper functioning of the immune system.

DID YOU KNOW?

High-quality Chinese and Japanese green teas should be steeped in cooler water (about 160°F). Steeping it too long will result in a bitter brew.

34

SUPERMANGO

2 SERVINGS

INGREDIENTS

1 mango, peeled and cut into pieces
Juice of 4 oranges
Juice of 1/2 lime
1/4 cup (60 ml) plain yogurt

PREPARATION

In a blender, or with a hand blender, purée all ingredients until smooth. Drink fresh!

HEALTH BENEFITS

Mango and orange are excellent sources of vitamins to kick-start the day, while lime is a powerful antiseptic.

35

GREEN TEA & KIWI

1 SERVING

INGREDIENTS

1 cup (250 ml) green tea, brewed and chilled
2 kiwis, peeled
Juice of 1 lemon
1 tsp cane syrup
1/2 cup (125 ml) crushed ice

PREPARATION

To prepare the green tea, infuse 1-1/2 tsp green tea leaves in 1 cup (250 ml) boiling water for 1 to 5 minutes.

In a blender, or with a hand blender, pulse all ingredients until smooth. Serve immediately.

HEALTH BENEFITS

The tannins in green tea help burn fat, while the polyphenols it contains lower blood sugar levels. Caffeine also helps the body burn more calories and has a diuretic effect. Besides water, tea is the only naturally calorie-free beverage.

36

COOL CUCUMBER & APPLE

2 SERVINGS

INGREDIENTS

1 red apple, cored, peeled, and quartered
1/2 cucumber, peeled and cut into cylinders
1 cup (250 ml) green grapes
8 fresh mint leaves

PREPARATION

In a blender, or with a hand blender, pulse all ingredients until smooth. Serve.

HEALTH BENEFITS

Cucumber is a powerful purifier that helps relieve arthritis pain by eliminating toxins like uric acid.

37

SUNNY CITRUS SORBET

1 SERVING

INGREDIENTS

1 orange, peeled and segmented
1 grapefruit, peeled and segmented
1/2 cup (125 ml) almond milk
2 tbsp orange sherbet
Juice of 1 lemon
1 tsp cane syrup or honey

PREPARATION

In a blender, or with a hand blender, purée all ingredients until smooth and creamy. Serve.

HEALTH BENEFITS

All fruit is good for the skin, especially citrus fruit. The vitamin C in citrus plays a part in the production of collagen, which firms and strengthens the skin. It also improves microcirculation, giving the skin a healthy glow.

38

GO GO GOJI!

2 SERVINGS

INGREDIENTS

1/2 banana
1 cup (250 ml) fresh or frozen raspberries
2 tbsp goji berries
1 orange, peeled and cut into pieces
2 tbsp sesame seeds
1 tbsp cane syrup or honey
1-1/2 tsp maca powder or ginseng (optional)

PREPARATION

In a blender, or with a hand blender, purée all ingredients until smooth. Serve.

HEALTH BENEFITS

This smoothie provides 45% of the recommended daily intake of calcium: the sesame seeds provide 28%, and the rest comes from the orange (6%), the goji berries (6%), the raspberries (4%), and the banana (1%). Maca, also called Peruvian ginger, stimulates the immune system and relieves stress.

DID YOU KNOW?

Although it's widely grown in Asia, one particular variety of ginseng is cultivated in parts of North America, mainly in Ontario and British Columbia, Canada, and in the American state of Wisconsin.

39

ORANGE, AVOCADO & BANANA

2 SERVINGS

INGREDIENTS

1 banana
1 small avocado, peeled and pitted
1/4 cup (60 ml) plain yogurt
1 cup (250 ml) vanilla soy milk
Zest of 1 orange
1 tbsp honey

PREPARATION

In a blender, or with a hand blender, purée all ingredients until smooth. Serve.

HEALTH BENEFITS

Avocado is creamy, rich, and loaded with health-giving unsaturated fats. It also slows digestion and helps prevent a spike in blood sugar after a meal.

40

CLASSIC STRAWBERRY BANANA

2 SERVINGS

INGREDIENTS

2 cups (500 ml) strawberries, cut into pieces
2 bananas, cut into pieces
1 cup (250 ml) plain yogurt
2 tbsp real maple syrup
Juice of 1/2 lemon
A few fresh mint leaves

PREPARATION

In a blender, or with a hand blender, purée all ingredients until smooth. Serve.

HEALTH BENEFITS

Strawberries are loaded with vitamin C, which acts as a diuretic, improves intestinal transit, and facilitates digestion. Bananas are high in fiber and promote normal bowel function.

41

MELLOW CRANBERRY

2 SERVINGS

INGREDIENTS

1 cup (250 ml) fresh cranberries
1 tbsp honey
1/4 cup (60 ml) water
2 pears, left unpeeled, cored and cut into pieces
1/2 cup (125 ml) crushed ice

PREPARATION

In a small pot, combine cranberries, honey, and water. Cover and cook for 15 to 20 minutes over low heat. Chill mixture before blending.

In a blender, or with a hand blender, purée all ingredients until smooth. Serve immediately.

HEALTH BENEFITS

Cranberries are the best natural remedy for urinary tract infections, and they also help lower cholesterol levels. The boron in pears raises estrogen levels in menopausal women.

42

SAVORY CHERVIL

2 SERVINGS

INGREDIENTS

1 cup (250 ml) baby spinach
1 cup (250 ml) chicken stock
2 tbsp 15% cream
1/2 cup (125 ml) fresh chervil, chopped
Juice of 1/2 lemon
Salt and freshly ground pepper

PREPARATION

In the microwave, wilt spinach for 30 seconds in 2 tbsp water. Let cool.

In a blender, or with a hand blender, purée all ingredients until smooth. Season with salt and pepper and serve.

HEALTH BENEFITS

Fresh chervil possesses diuretic properties.

DID YOU KNOW?

Instead of drying fresh chervil for future use, keep it in the freezer: dried chervil loses its flavor over time.

43

CHOCOBERRY

2 SERVINGS

INGREDIENTS

1/2 cup (125 ml) blueberries
10 black cherries, pitted
1/2 banana
1/4 cup (60 ml) plain yogurt
1/2 cup (125 ml) chocolate milk

PREPARATION

In a blender, or with a hand blender, purée all ingredients until smooth. Serve.

44

FRUITSATION

4 TO 6 SERVINGS

INGREDIENTS

2 cups (500 ml) soy milk
1 large fresh or frozen banana
1 mango, peeled and cut into pieces
2 kiwis, peeled
1 cup (250 ml) strawberries, hulled
2 peaches or nectarines, pitted
3 plums, pitted
2 cups (500 ml) pineapple, peeled, cored, and cut into pieces
Crushed ice

PREPARATION

In a blender, or with a hand blender, purée soy milk and fruit until smooth. Add crushed ice and pulse until smooth. Serve immediately.

45

TOMATO TURMERIC

1 SERVING

INGREDIENTS

1 tsp turmeric
1 tbsp olive oil
1/2 cup (125 ml) tomato juice
1/2 cup (125 ml) carrot juice
1 pinch black pepper

PREPARATION

In a large glass, combine turmeric and olive oil, and stir until well blended. Add tomato juice, carrot juice, and pepper, and mix well. Serve immediately.

HEALTH BENEFITS

Turmeric is one of nature's most powerful healers, and has shown promise in the prevention and treatment of cancer! Studies have proven that combining piperine (found in black pepper) with curcumin (the main pigment in turmeric) aids the absorption of curcumin into the bloodstream, protecting the body's cells from oxidative stress.

DID YOU KNOW?

Because of its vivid orange-yellow color, turmeric has been used for centuries in many Asian countries to dye fabric and in India to tint the skin for traditional ceremonies.

85

46

THE RED, WHITE & BLUE

4 SERVINGS

INGREDIENTS

1/2 cup (125 ml) milk
1 cup (250 ml) berries of your choice
(strawberries, blueberries, raspberries, etc.)
1/2 cup (125 ml) plain yogurt
1 tbsp real maple syrup

PREPARATION

In a blender, or with a hand blender, purée all ingredients until smooth. Serve.

HEALTH BENEFITS

Red and blue berries contain anthocyanins, naturally occurring compounds that scientific research suggests may contribute to lowering blood sugar by stimulating insulin production.

47

1, 2, 3, GO!

4 SERVINGS

INGREDIENTS

1 cup (250 ml) plain soy milk
1 cup (250 ml) orange juice
1 banana
2 mangoes, peeled and cut into cubes
1/2 cup (125 ml) soft tofu

PREPARATION

In a blender, or with a hand blender, purée ingredients until smooth. Serve immediately.

HEALTH BENEFITS

After exercising, it's important to eat foods containing beneficial protein, like milk, tofu, or other soy products. These foods also contain vitamins and calcium, which are absorbed slowly by the body and help active people maintain a steady energy level throughout the day.

DID YOU KNOW?

Soft tofu, also known as silken tofu, should be stored in water and will keep in the refrigerator for 7 to 10 days. Change the tofu water daily.

48

ELEGANT MELON

1 SERVING

INGREDIENTS

1 cup (250 ml) cantaloupe, peeled and cut into cubes
1 tsp dried lavender flowers
1/2 cup (125 ml) almond milk
1 tsp honey

PREPARATION

In a blender, or with a hand blender, purée all ingredients until smooth. Serve.

DID YOU KNOW?

The Ancient Romans used lavender for cooking, scenting the air, and bathing. Its name, in fact, comes from the Latin verb *lavare*, which means "to wash."

49

THE GOOD START

1 SERVING

INGREDIENTS

1 cup (250 ml) milk
1 frozen banana
1 tbsp creamy peanut butter

PREPARATION

In a blender, or with a hand blender, pulse all ingredients until smooth. Serve immediately.

HEALTH BENEFITS

As long as you aren't allergic to peanuts, this quick and easy breakfast smoothie will start the day off on the right foot and it requires just a few simple ingredients! Peanut butter is a great way to incorporate protein and healthy fat into your breakfast, and one tablespoon has just 85 calories, most of which come from healthy fat, protein, and carbohydrates that the body needs to provide energy throughout the day.

CAR
23
CAR

50

PURELY PEACH

1 SERVING

INGREDIENTS

1/2 cup (125 ml) plain probiotic yogurt
1 peach, pitted and cut into pieces
1/2 cup (125 ml) crushed ice

PREPARATION

In a blender, or with a hand blender, purée all ingredients until smooth. Drink immediately.

HEALTH BENEFITS

Highly digestible and excellent for the intestinal flora, probiotic yogurt helps reduce stomach bloating and gives the waistline more definition in a matter of days.

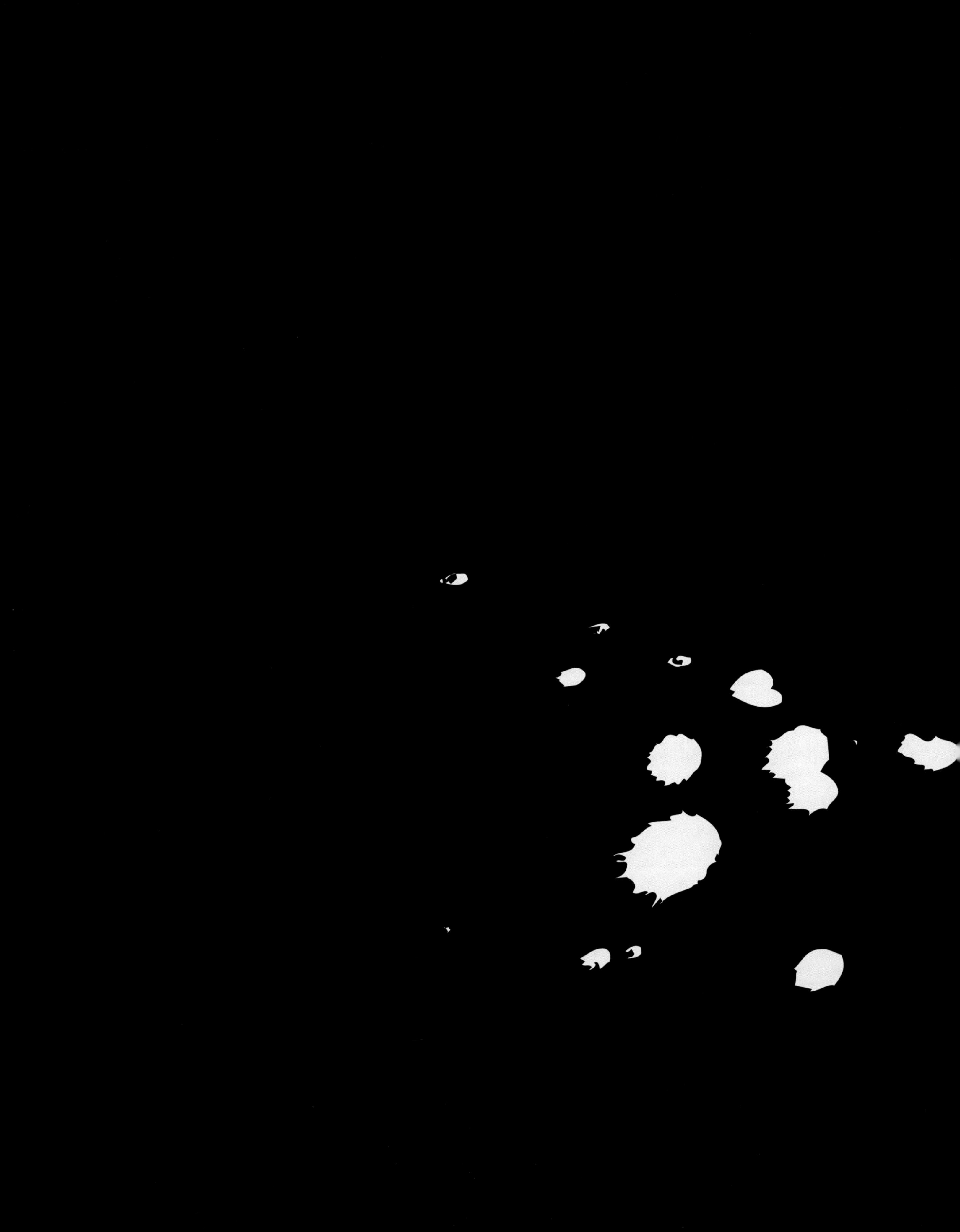

51

APPLE, RASPBERRY & SOY

1 SERVING

INGREDIENTS

1/2 cup (125 ml) soy milk
1 apple, cored and cut into pieces
1/2 cup (125 ml) raspberries
1/2 cup (125 ml) soft tofu
2 tbsp oat bran
1 tbsp real maple syrup

PREPARATION

In a blender, or with a hand blender, purée all ingredients until smooth. Drink immediately.

52

POWER SMOOTHIE

2 SERVINGS

DID YOU KNOW?

The word smoothie has been part of the American vocabulary since the beginning of the 20th century, when it was used by the Adler Company of Connecticut as a name for girdles and brassieres!

INGREDIENTS

1 cup (250 ml) spinach (or mâche)
4 sprigs parsley
1/2 cup (125 ml) water
1 apple, cored and cut into pieces
1/2 banana

PREPARATION

In a small pot, wilt spinach and parsley in water. Save water and let greens and water cool in the refrigerator.

When cool, purée greens, water, and remaining ingredients until smooth. Serve.

HEALTH BENEFITS

Did you know that just 1/2 cup (125 ml) of spinach provides the entire recommended daily intake of vitamin K, which is essential to bone health? Vitamin K deficiency can lead to reduced bone density and increase the risk of fractures in post-menopausal women and women over 60.

53

GRAPE, YOGURT & BANANA

2 SERVINGS

INGREDIENTS

2 cups (500 ml) red grapes
1 cup (250 ml) plain yogurt
1 banana

PREPARATION

In a blender, or with a hand blender, purée all ingredients until smooth and creamy. Serve.

HEALTH BENEFITS

The flavonoids in grapes that give them their red color are powerful antioxidant pigments, which help slow the effects of aging and promote the regeneration of the cardiovascular system. Because these antioxidants bind to the collagen in the arterial walls, they help strengthen and increase flexibility in the arteries as well as the veins and capillaries.

54

AFTER-SKI SMOOTHIE

2 SERVINGS

DID YOU KNOW?

Allspice is the dried, unripened fruit of the *Pimenta dioica* tree. The flavor of the small, red-brown, pea-sized berry evokes a combination of clove, cinnamon, and nutmeg.

INGREDIENTS

1 apple, cored and cut into pieces
1 banana
1/2 cup (125 ml) vanilla yogurt
1/2 cup (125 ml) milk
1/2 tsp allspice
1/4 tsp cinnamon

PREPARATION

In a blender, or with a hand blender, purée all ingredients until smooth. Serve.

55

ESPRESSO GOOD

1 SERVING

INGREDIENTS

1 short espresso, about 1/4 cup (60 ml)
1/2 cup (125 ml) crushed ice
1 banana
1/2 cup (125 ml) vanilla yogurt
1 tbsp real maple syrup
1/2 cup (125 ml) milk

PREPARATION

Pour coffee into a blender and add crushed ice. Blend until coffee is thoroughly chilled. Add remaining ingredients and purée until smooth. Serve.

DID YOU KNOW?

It's a common misconception that a small espresso contains more caffeine than filtered coffee. Although espresso does have more caffeine per ounce than other coffee beverages, its typical serving size is much smaller: one espresso contains 80 to 150 mg of caffeine, while one standard cup (240 ml) of drip coffee contains 95 to 200 mg.

56

THE TURQUOISE

1 SERVING

INGREDIENTS

1 kiwi, peeled and halved
1/2 cup (125 ml) lemon probiotic yogurt
1/4 cup (60 ml) wheatgrass powder
1 tbsp canola oil
1 tbsp ground flaxseeds
1 tbsp honey
1/2 cup (125 ml) crushed ice

PREPARATION

In a blender, or with a hand blender, purée all ingredients until smooth. Drink immediately.

HEALTH BENEFITS

Wheatgrass powder fortifies the immune system and is rich in minerals, vitamins, proteins, and enzymes. It also contains chlorophyll, which flushes out accumulated toxins and helps cleanse the liver, lungs, and colon.

57

Coconut Lychee

1 SERVING

INGREDIENTS

4 canned or 8 fresh lychees, pitted
1 banana
1/4 cup (60 ml) coconut milk
1/2 cup (125 ml) vanilla yogurt
Juice of 1/2 lime
1 piece fresh ginger (about 1/2 inch), peeled
1/2 cup (125 ml) milk

PREPARATION

In a blender, or with a hand blender, purée all ingredients until smooth. Serve.

58

SOY APRICOT

1 SERVING

DID YOU KNOW?

In India, sesame seeds are a symbol of immortality.

INGREDIENTS

1 cup (250 ml) soy milk
4 fresh apricots, pitted and cut into pieces
2 pinches black pepper
2 tbsp sesame seeds
1/2 tsp fresh thyme leaves, finely chopped
1 tsp sesame seeds (for garnish)
1 slice lemon

PREPARATION

In a blender, or with a hand blender, purée soy milk, apricots, pepper, and 2 tbsp sesame seeds until smooth.

For garnish, combine sesame seeds and 1 tbsp thyme. To prepare glass, coat the rims with lemon juice and then dip in sesame seed and thyme mixture. Pour smoothie into glass and garnish with fresh thyme.

HEALTH BENEFITS

The more intense the color of the apricot, the richer it is in provitamin A (or beta-carotene), which protects cells against free radicals thanks to its antioxidant properties. This provitamin also plays an important role in skin health by regulating the growth of skin cells and improving epidermal collagen levels. Sesame's sesamin increases the amount of vitamin E available in the blood and tissues, which helps reduce inflammation. It's also involved in the body's protection against ultraviolet B radiation.

59

WAKE UP!

2 SERVINGS

INGREDIENTS

1/2 cup (125 ml) blueberries
1/2 banana
1 cup (250 ml) soy milk
1/4 cup (60 ml) plain yogurt
1 tbsp ground flaxseeds
1 tsp spirulina powder

PREPARATION

In a blender, or with a hand blender, purée all ingredients until smooth. Serve.

HEALTH BENEFITS

Start your day with this delicious combination of antioxidant-rich berries, flaxseeds, and spirulina. Spirulina is a complete protein and contains all of the essential amino acids. A true breakfast of champions!

DID YOU KNOW?

Because spirulina is rich in nutrients and can be cultivated anywhere in the world, it's used in many countries as a dietary supplement to fight malnutrition.

60

FRUIT, FLAX & BRAN

2 SERVINGS

INGREDIENTS

1 red apple, cored and cut into pieces
1 cup (250 ml) strawberries, hulled
1 cup (250 ml) watermelon, seeded and cut into pieces
2 tbsp oat or wheat bran
2 tsp ground flaxseeds
1 cup (250 ml) crushed ice

PREPARATION

In a blender, or with a hand blender, purée all ingredients until smooth. If the mixture is too thick, add a bit of water.

HEALTH BENEFITS

This smoothie has a very subtle sweetness, and is incredibly rich in fiber, vitamins, and omega-3 fatty acids thanks to the flaxseeds it contains. Oat bran is a weight loss ally that, while promoting healthy digestion, limits calorie absorption. It also helps prevent the onset of diabetes, reduces the risk of colon cancer, and lowers cholesterol levels.

INGREDIENTS INDEX

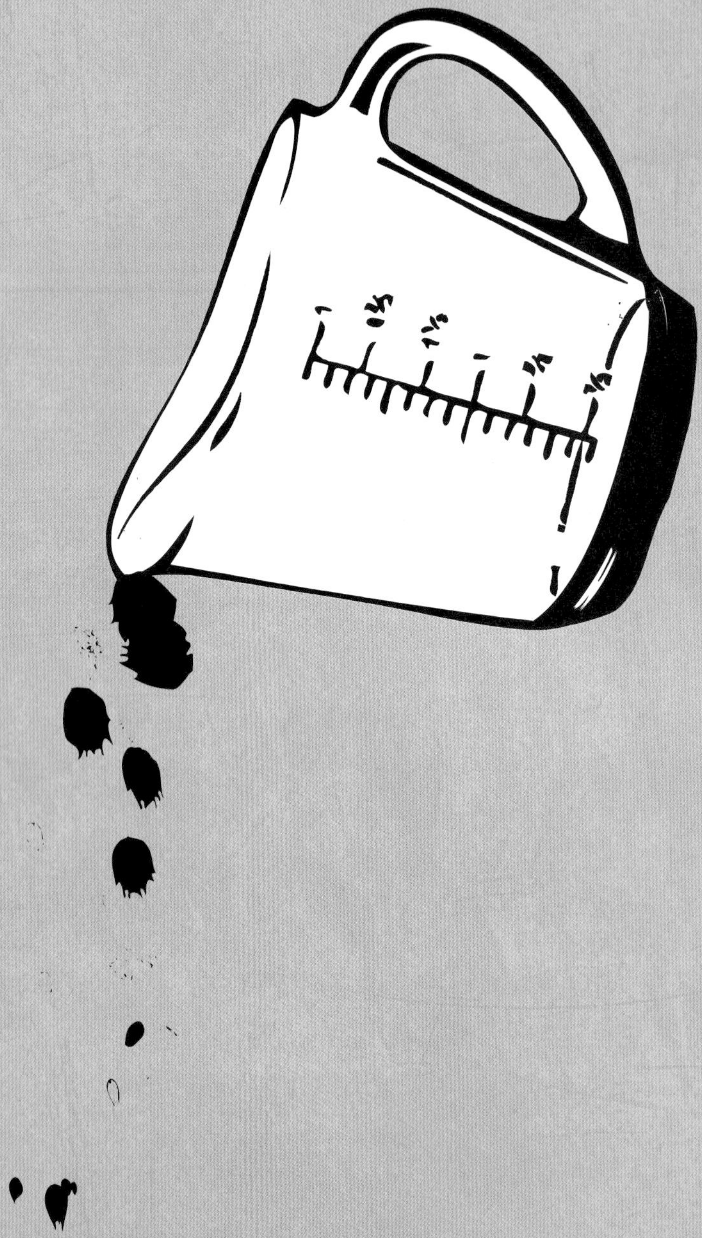

CONVERSION CHART

1 dl	10 cl	100 ml
1 tablespoon		15 ml
1 teaspoon		5 ml
1 oz.		30 ml
1 cup		250 ml
4 cups		1 l
1/2 cup		125 ml
1/4 cup		60 ml
1/3 cup		80 ml
1 lb		450 g
2 lbs		900 g
2.2 lbs		1 kg
400°F	200°C	T/7
350°F	175°C	T/6
300°F	150°C	T/5

Volume Conversion
* Approximate values

1 cup (250 ml) crumbled cheese	150 g
1 cup (250 ml) all-purpose flour	115 g
1 cup (250 ml) white sugar	200 g
1 cup (250 ml) brown sugar	220 g
1 cup (250 ml) butter	230 g
1 cup (250 ml) oil	215 g
1 cup (250 ml) canned tomatoes	250 g

CORTLAND
MC IN TOSH
LO BO

NOTES

60

IN THE SAME COLLECTION

THE WORLD'S 60 BEST
SALADS
PERIOD.

THE WORLD'S 60 BEST
PASTA SAUCES
PERIOD.

THE WORLD'S 60 BEST
BURGERS
PERIOD.

THE WORLD'S 60 BEST
LUNCHES
PERIOD.

THE WORLD'S 60 BEST
RECIPES FOR STUDENTS
PERIOD.

THE WORLD'S 60 BEST
PIZZAS
PERIOD.

THE WORLD'S 60 BEST
GRATINS
PERIOD.

THE WORLD'S 60 BEST
STUFFED DISHES
PERIOD.

THE WORLD'S 60 BEST
SOUPS
PERIOD.

THE WORLD'S 60 BEST
STEWS
PERIOD.

Discover our upcoming books and much more!

WWW.FACEBOOK.COM/THEWORLDS60BEST